YOUR BES

The Secret to Being
Fiercely Focused

How to Have More Energy, Less Stress, and Get More Done by Tackling Your Tolerations

MICHAEL E. ANGIER

Published by Success Networks International, Inc.
Spring Hill, Florida 34609-9509
www.SuccessNet.org

ISBN: 9781798111086

Editorial Reviews

"If you've ever been challenged by overwhelm or felt nibbled to death by all the nagging little things that distract and annoy you, this book is for you. Michael Angier is a master at coaching you through the process of identifying and eliminating your Tolerations. The result is a lot more done—faster and with greater ease. Never think that tolerations are ever eternally eliminated. It takes mindful attention."

—Lorraine Lane
www.Lanebc.com

"I first learned the term 'Tolerations' from Michael as far back as 2006. Freeing yourself of tolerations was unique then and still is today. Engaging in the practice of "clearing the decks" that Michael teaches will free up your mental energy. And you can use your newfound energy to have more fun, avoid stress and feel more empowered about your life. Learn from Michael and then try it out. You won't be disappointed."

—Shane Fielder
www.SamuraiInnovation.com

"I don't know who said it first, but it's true: 'You get what you tolerate!' If you are dealing with simple stuff now that you would rather not deal with, Michael Angier can help you. Michael has really helped me throughout the years on a personal and professional level. When he taught me the basics in this book, I was able to significantly change my life. I eliminated people and activities that weren't helping me improve in any way. Through this book, The Secret to Being Fully Focused, *Michael can guide you, too, so you can identify those things that are truly nagging you, help you eliminate them, and allow you to focus on what is really important in this beautiful thing called life."*

—Dr. Rejina Hendricksen

Table of Contents

Introduction

"The journey of a thousand miles begins with a single step."

—Lao Tzu

Many books have been written about how you can be more successful, live a better life and achieve your dreams. Most of this advice falls into the strategies and tactics that you need to employ in order to win the game.

But much less has been written about what you need to *not* do. Instead of skills, talents and knowledge you need to acquire, there are also things you need to discard. Things that sap your energy, distract you, take away your focus and rob you of joy, peace and happiness.

I call these Tolerations—things you tolerate, but should not.

Tolerations are anything that detracts from your enjoyment, causes frustration, distracts you, irritates you, aggravates you or annoys you. They're things that are broken, worn out, unclean, ragged, too slow, stinky, over-complicated, outdated, cluttered or disheveled.

They clutter your mind and your life. They are deadly detractors and they make it harder to achieve what you

Michael E. Angier

want—even causing you to be *unclear* about what you want—and where you want to go.

Tolerations are sneaky. They affect you often without your awareness. But they do their dirty mischief nonetheless.

This book is intended to make you aware of how much Tolerations are costing you and how they may have kept you from living your best life. It will also show you how much more smoothly your life will run when you learn to identify and eradicate them—especially the well-hidden ones.

The goal of this book is to help you master "Toleration Freedom".

It's a simple concept. But don't allow its simplicity to cause you to think it's not life-changingly powerful.

I can tell you that it has changed my life from being at the effect of things that happen to me to being much more at cause. From being hundreds of thousands of dollars in debt to being debt free. From working for a business to having a business work for me.

All of this was substantially impacted by my attempt to achieve Toleration Freedom. I've also seen it work for many others. And it can work for you, too.

If you want to have less stress, more clarity, better focus and increased energy, I promise you will benefit from mastering Toleration Freedom.

Let's get started.

Chapter 1
Your Best Life

> *"We all have two choices: We can make a living or we can design a life."*
>
> —Jim Rohn

Are You Seeking Your Best Life?

Before we get into the heart of Toleration Freedom, let's take a look at our objectives.

If you are reading this, I assume you want a better life. You want to improve on where you are. Maybe a little. Maybe a lot.

Regardless of where you find yourself at this point in time—and regardless of your age—you can certainly improve. After all, the biggest room in the world is the room for improvement.

You may be wanting to take your comfortable life and simply make it better. Or maybe your life is a train wreck.

Either way, we have to start with the end in mind.

It's important to acknowledge where you are, but there will be plenty of time for that. What's more important is getting clear on where you're going.

Michael E. Angier

Your best life doesn't just happen. It doesn't automatically unfold, and it's not given to you. You have to design and create your best life yourself. Because if you don't, other people and outside circumstances will do it for you. And do you know what other people and outside circumstances have planned for you? Hardly anything at all.

What's Your Life Vision?

No doubt you have some idea about what your Best Life looks like. I assume you have some goals—some things you want to accomplish or experience before you make your departure from planet Earth.

Have you ever envisioned in great detail how you would like to have your life unfold? Do you see it? Can you taste it? Do you believe it?

Your Best Life Vision is the subject of another book. But suffice to say that the clearer you can become on all the things you want in your life—and the reason why—the easier it will be to do what you need to do to achieve it.

The strategy of identifying and eliminating Tolerations will allow you to achieve your best life more easily, and you will have more fun in the process.

We all want to be happy, and I personally believe we are happiest when we are in pursuit of our highest and best.

For now, let me share with you, in general terms, what I mean by your Best Life. It should give you some ideas for your Best Life Vision—or improvements on it.

---

*"Your Best Life is a life
with no regrets."*

It's a tall order, but I think your Best Life is a life without regrets.

Your Best Life is a life by design, not default.

I think you should build a life you don't need a vacation from. Not that you won't *take* vacations, but you won't *need* them. Because your vocation is your avocation. And it's not a struggle; it's a wiggle.

---

*Your Best Life requires
your best self.*

Your Best Life requires your best self. If you want your life to get better, *you* have to get better. I'm guessing that's why you're reading this book.

For me it means rising to a calling instead of an alarm clock. I get up when I *want* to get up, and very rarely do I use an alarm clock. It is possible.

I believe your Best Life is a life of clarity, purpose, passion and prosperity. A life designed around your values, principles and intentions.

Simply put—a life on your terms. You get to design, define, create and live Your Best Life.

Michael E. Angier

Top Seven Results of Living Your Best Life

The following seven benefits are what I consider to be the biggest payoffs for living a life well lived.

1. Significance & Meaning

2. Time, Location & Financial Freedom

3. Happiness, Fun & Adventure

4. Purpose & Integrity

5. Confidence & Self-esteem

6. Rich Relationships

7. Health, Fitness & Vitality

Sounds worthwhile, yes?

Your full and unique potential is always unknown. But certainly worth going for, don't you think? Who can count the number of apples in a single apple seed?

"Death is not the greatest loss in life. The greatest loss is what dies inside us while we live."
—Norman Cousins

The Path to Your Best Life

The illustration that follows shows what I believe to be the best path to your best life—however you might define it. The bottom four tiers are foundational. The top three are much more dynamic. But they should stand in support of your core values, purpose, mission and vision.

Tasks

Projects

Goals

Vision

Mission

Purpose

Core Values

Your Path to Your Best Life

"Life should not be a journey to the grave with the intention of arriving safely in a pretty and well-preserved body, but rather to skid in broadside in a cloud of smoke, thoroughly used up, totally worn out, and loudly proclaiming 'Wow, what a ride!' "

—Hunter S. Thompson

My belief is that you can do anything in this life. But you can't do *everything*. And that's why it's so important to choose your goals and projects wisely. And to base them on the foundational steps of core values, purpose, mission and vision. Otherwise, you are making choices and spending your precious time and energy on your own or others' whims.

These foundational steps are not within the scope of this book, but I strongly encourage you to think carefully about them. Getting clear on your core values, your mission and purpose, and having a clear vision for your life will help you to avoid regrets and feel like you invested your life in the best way you could.

The bottom line is that unless you invest the time, energy and money in creating a life you truly want, you're going to be spending a lot of time and effort supporting a life you *don't* want.

"A successful day: to learn something new; to laugh at least 10 times; to lift someone up; to make progress on a worthy goal; to practice peace and patience; to do something nice for yourself and another; to appreciate and be grateful for all your blessings."
—Michael Angier

Action Steps

1. Begin to list the components of your best life. Describe your life in terms of your income, health, relationships,

environment, home, career, family, attitude, location, hobbies, travel, etc. This is a time to think big. It doesn't cost anything to dream big. The important thing here is to start thinking clearly and in great detail.

2. Please also consider this home-study course on discovering and clarifying your core values. To find out more, go to www.YourCoreValues.com

Thousands of people have taken this course and benefited from the process.

"Starve your distractions;
feed your focus."

Michael E. Angier

*"Clutter-clearing is
modern-day alchemy."*

—Denise Linn

Chapter 2
Defining Your Tolerations

"You will never change
what you tolerate."
—Joel Osteen

What Exactly Are Tolerations?

Tolerations are anything that detracts from your enjoyment, causes frustration, distracts you, irritates you, aggravates you or annoys you. They're things that are broken, worn out, unclean, ragged, too slow, stinky, over-complicated, outdated, cluttered or disheveled.

That's not a complete list, but I think you get the picture.

When you're struggling, too often you just try harder, or you work longer or you try new things when all you have to do is let go of some of the baggage you're dragging around.

We all have some of these things in our life. But we don't need to tolerate them. Doing so makes our life less enjoyable—sometimes downright unbearable.

They may seem like small, innocuous, even normal, things to put up with. But in the aggregate—taken together— they rob you of your energy, enjoyment, focus and satisfaction.

11

Michael E. Angier

The editor of a magazine I once owned used a phrase I have never heard anyone else use. When referring to a large number of niggly problems, he would say, "it's like being nibbled to death by ducks". And that's kind of what it feels like when you let your Tolerations pile up.

One of the books I've written is *The Achievement Code: The 3C Formula for Getting What You Truly Want*. And the three C's are Clarity, Concentration and Consistency.

In my extensive research, I found that all three of these C's are necessary to be successful. If you're not making the progress you would like to be making, the solution can be found in one of these three areas. And I see Tolerations as being one of the biggest killers of clarity, concentration and consistency.

Mastering the identification and elimination of Tolerations in your life will substantially upgrade the quality of your life. You will have more freedom, joy, happiness and peace. Guaranteed!

This could very well be the missing piece of your success and satisfaction journey that you've been looking for.

"Your personal values are the best compass for your unique journey."
—Chris Hutchinson

Examples of Tolerations

Tolerations come in many shapes and sizes. Some have a big impact on you and others only a little. But taken together, they add up to be attention, focus and energy suckers. They all take their toll.

You'll find them in your car, your house, your office, your wardrobe and your finances, to name a few places.

It's the ugly green tile in the guest bathroom that you've put off replacing.

It could be credit card debt.

Sometimes it's excessive clutter in the office.

The dent in the car's passenger door.

A floor that squeaks.

A boss that's rude, demanding or unprofessional.

That extra 15 pounds you've been carrying for 4 years.

Your cell phone battery that has to be charged several times a day.

A dresser that's packed tight with clothes—some of which haven't been worn in years.

A tenant who consistently pays the rent late.

In short, a Toleration is anything that bothers you, is inconvenient, slow, aggravating, makes you go, "yuck" or causes you to wince. It's anything that offends your sensibility—but for whatever reason, you've allowed it. It

13

hasn't risen to the level that you say it must be fixed. Or, more accurately, you haven't elevated it to be worthy of eradication.

The Principle of Vacuum

It's a matter of making room for what you want by getting rid of what you don't. If your life is filled with things that no longer serve you, there's no room for the things that can.

And just like useless things that take up space in your closets and garage, Tolerations take up space in your mind.

And just like useless things that take up space in your closets and garage, Tolerations take up space in your mind—they take up space and they drain your energy.

Everybody Has Tolerations

We all have things in our life that, at best, don't serve us. And many of these things actually detract from the quality and satisfaction of our lives.

Maybe not all the time, but we all get distracted, we lose focus, have insufficient energy, get frustrated and are unclear. We feel overwhelmed, put up with less than we deserve, and we long for a simpler existence.

Toleration identification and elimination can fix that. Your life can—and should—run more smoothly. You deserve it.

You'll Find Them Everywhere

Scientists tell us that there's a small part of our brain (located near the brain stem) that governs our ability to focus. It's called the Reticular Activation System. And apparently, if the RAS wasn't there, we would be incapable of concentration because we would be distracted by every tiny thing in our environment and in our thinking.

The fly buzzing in the next room, the A/C fan coming on and the bird flying outside our window would become so distracting as to render us numb and ineffective.

Conversely, what we think about, what we want and what has our interest directs the RAS to filter non-relevant data and notice what *is* relevant.

You've seen this process work when you started thinking about buying a certain type of car. Up until then, you never before noticed so many of these cars and now they seem to be everywhere. That's your RAS working for you—drawing your attention to what it thinks is relevant to you.

And now that you know what Tolerations are—and how diabolical they can be—your RAS will find them in lots of places.

Goals Can Come from Tolerations

Knowing what you want often comes from knowing what you *don't* want. Tolerations can be the genesis of big, important goals. Some Tolerations are big enough to warrant setting goals and creating projects to eliminate them.

*"An exceptional company is the
one that gets all the little
details right. And the people
out on the front line, they know
when things are not going
right, and they know when
things need to be improved.
And if you listen to them, you
can soon improve all those
niggly things which turns an
average company into an
exceptional company."*

—Sir Richard Branson

Action Steps

Start making a list of potential Tolerations you may be putting up with. Carry your list with you and add to it as you recognize Tolerations. Don't worry about how to handle them, this step is just to identify them. Naming them is the first step. It starts the elimination process.

Tolerations List

P = Priority

1 – Serious impediment, must eliminate

2 – Important to eradicate

3 – Bothersome, but tolerable (at least for now)

Date	Tolerations	P
2/25/19	15 pounds overweight—clothes don't fit very well or at all	1
2/25/19	Back door hinges rusty and door hard to open	2

Michael E. Angier

Chapter 3
Raising Your Standards

"Excellence is never an accident. It is always the result of high intention, sincere effort, and intelligent execution; it represents the wise choice of many alternatives—choice, not chance, determines your destiny."

—Aristotle

Why are Successful People Successful?

Since I was a teenager, I've been an ardent student of personal and professional development. I've interviewed, read about, watched and listened to some of the most successful, prosperous and effective people I could find. I'm always looking for the common denominators of people who consistently win.

I've also studied *un*successful people. Because they have something to teach us as well. It's just that there are no honorariums for people to get up and tell how they didn't do it.

Michael E. Angier

There are many, many attributes of winners that differ from those who—well, let's just say, don't live up to their potential.

One attribute of successful people is simply not settling for less than they feel they deserve. They want things to be better *and* they're willing to take the actions necessary to make them so.

> *One attribute of successful people is simply not settling for less than they feel they deserve.*

The great American inventor, Charles Kettering, invented the automobile electric starter after getting injured by a starter crank. The crank didn't disengage immediately when the engine kicked over and when it spun around, it broke his arm.

More than a little annoyed, he decided there had to be a better way than hand cranking the engine from the front of the car. And he found it. Thank you, Charles. We're all grateful for our electric starters, aren't we?

There's no guarantee you will invent anything that's as big a breakthrough as Kettering invented—but you might.

> *"It is in your moments of decision that your destiny is shaped."*

Is it Really a Decision?

Yes, I believe we can raise our standards by consciously choosing to do so. And zapping Tolerations is a great path to getting there.

It's a decision to not accept less than you deserve and the thousands of decisions that follow that will make it a reality.

I know that I have higher standards than I used to have before taking on Toleration executions. I'm a little embarrassed when I recall having put up with some of the things I tolerated.

Many years ago, I drove a car around for weeks that had a driver's side door that wouldn't open from the inside. Yup, I had to roll the window down, reach out and use the outside door handle to open the door.

When I went to get the car inspected, they wouldn't pass it unless the door worked properly. They couldn't fix it just then, and before I could get it repaired, I ended up getting stopped by a State Trooper for having an uninspected vehicle. And I had to pay a steep fine.

Today, I wouldn't tolerate something like that at all. No way.

But even though I've gotten very good at the recognizing and eliminating of Tolerations, they still show up. They're like weeds in the garden; they just creep in.

Michael E. Angier

*"Diligence is the mother
of good luck."*
—Benjamin Franklin

A few years back I realized I had made some good progress in raising my standards. I'd been working with Tolerations and their defeat for over ten years and a decision I made regarding our sailboat made me realize how far I'd come.

It was back when we lived in Vermont. Early one spring, I asked Rick, the head of the shipyard crew, to replace the mooring light when they put the boat back in the water. It's a small light at the very top of the mast, which was 52 feet off the water—almost 60 feet from the ground when she was "on the hard".

Rick looked at me a little skeptically. He said they could do it, but he warned me that it would require the use of their crane and it would cost at least $100. He thought I might not want to spend that much to fix a $3 light that would only be used if we ever anchored in a non-designated mooring area—something we would only do in an emergency.

I thanked Rick for warning me of the expense, but said I wanted to do it anyway. I told him that things that didn't work bothered me. I further explained, "I've spent way too many years putting up with things that didn't work, or didn't work well. You see, my goal is to have a house, a car and a boat where everything works—and a wife that doesn't have to."

Rick chuckled a little, smiled, and said, "We'll take care of it, Mr. Angier." I smiled, too. This stuff really works—if you work it.

Yes, You Do Deserve It

Sometimes people don't feel deserving, and that's one of the reasons why it's hard to raise their standards. Hopefully, that's not you.

But just in case it is, let me tell you that you do deserve to have high standards and you do deserve to live Toleration Free. You do not have to earn the right to live a better life. If you're here, if you're breathing—you deserve it.

My belief is that the Universe tends to treat us about as well as we treat ourselves. So decide to treat yourself really well. Because Source Energy will respond in kind.

Respect yourself enough to say, "I deserve better." Because you do.

Where are Your Standards Lacking?

What area of your life have you settled for less than you should? Is it in your relationship with your mate? Is it at work? Your home? Your grooming? Your wardrobe? Your diet?

There's an old story about the three stages of alcoholism. First Stage: When a waiter brings you a drink and it has a fly in it, you simply send it back for a fresh drink—maybe even go to a different establishment. Second Stage: You flick the fly out and drink the drink (you don't want to wait for a fresh one). Third Stage: You reach down, and squeeze the fly in case he drank any, throw the fly away, and drink your drink.

We certainly don't want to live in the second or third stage of our life standards, do we?

It's worth some thinking time and journaling time to evaluate your standards and see where you need to spiff them up. Look at all the various areas and interactions in your life and make note of where you have settled for less than the best.

"The quality of a leader is reflected in the standards they set for themselves."
—Ray Kroc

Would You Like to Have a WINE Meeting?

One of the recommendations I often make to my business coaching clients is to conduct regular WINE meetings with their team. Yes, wine can be served, but that's not why they're called WINE meetings.

WINE stands for What Is Not Excellent. It's a chance to examine processes, systems, products, services and outcomes. By asking the question, "What is not excellent?" you can brainstorm ways to make them excellent—or at least better than they are currently.

Can You Just Say No?

I've found that as I have become more successful, there are far more opportunities presented to me than there used to be. You can't say yes to everything and, in fact, you have to get better at saying no. Raising your standards sometimes means saying no to the good, so you can say yes to the great.

Raising your standards sometimes means saying no to the good, so you can say yes to the great.

Action Steps

I suggest you have some WINE meetings with yourself, your mate, your friends, or a coach or mastermind partner. What about your life, your career, your personality, your finances is less than excellent?

Getting the right answers is much more probable when you have asked the right questions. Good questions get you to think well. And you will certainly find some Tolerations in the process.

The greatest lever for change is awareness.

Michael E. Angier

Chapter 4
The Cost of Tolerations

"Price is what you pay.
Value is what you get."
—Warren Buffett

How Big a Toll are They Taking?

Tolerations are spirit-sucking, energy-draining, attention-assaulting enemies of our joy, happiness and achievement.

The great football coach, Vince Lombardi, said, "Fatigue makes cowards of us all." And Tolerations tire us—mentally, physically and emotionally.

I don't mind being tired from doing productive, creative, even physical work. But I hate being tired from frustrations, obstructions and thwarted efforts. And Tolerations play a big role in that kind of fatigue.

Some Long-Term Effects of Tolerations

Unaddressed Tolerations cause . . .

- unfulfilled potential
- additional expenses
- stress
- unachieved goals
- irritation
- impatience

Michael E. Angier

- irascibility
- low energy
- poor health
- loss of peace and tranquility

If you don't address them, your lives spiral downward. If you do, life spirals upward. It's never static.

And isn't peace, joy and happiness what you all want in your life? Then why tolerate things that detract from that peace, joy and happiness?

Do You Ever Get Grouchy?

Look, we all get grumpy sometimes. But have you ever wondered why? Is it just that you're tired or hangry (hunger-induced grouchiness)? What causes you to be frustrated and short-tempered?

I believe a good deal of it is putting up with things you don't need to tolerate. Being grumpy or ill-tempered costs you—probably more than you realize. It doesn't do nice things to you, and it certainly doesn't make your relationships with others easier or more endearing.

"I have, with great intentionality, a demeanor that I hope is welcoming for people to not be afraid to talk to me or, you know, ask me a question."
—Emanuel Cleaver

Would You Like More Time?

The one thing that every person on the planet has an equal amount of—in any given day, week or month—is time. I had 24 hours yesterday and so did you. So did almost 8 billion other people.

So it all comes down to how you utilize the time you have. You want to spend more time doing things you want to do, and less time doing the things you *don't* want to do. No argument there, right?

So Tolerations that fall into the inconvenient, time-wasting, productivity-blocking categories clearly cost you in wasted time. Something that costs you five minutes a day is taking up 30 hours a year of your precious life. And it does the same next year, and the next . . .

Spending 15 minutes replacing, repairing, eliminating—or whatever it takes—not only frees up a lot of time, it's one less thing to nag at you. That's a darn good return on your time investment.

"Dost thou love life? Then do not squander time, for that is the stuff life is made of."
—Benjamin Franklin

Be Here Now

Whether you're working or playing, relaxing or exercising, you want to be present. And it's impossible to be fully present if you're distracted and unfocused.

Michael E. Angier

The truth is you can only consciously think about one thing at a time. You can switch back and forth between one thought and another *very* fast—fast enough for it to *seem* like you are holding multiple thoughts, but you're really not.

Being fully present allows you to have more peace. And we all want more of that, right?

The game then, is to whittle away at anything that detracts from your ability to focus and your experience of peace. Identifying and eliminating Tolerations will do that.

You Get What You Tolerate

One of the areas to take a close look at is how other people treat you. You can't make people respect you, but you don't have to accept being *dis*respected. You have to be very careful what you tolerate from others because you are teaching them how to treat you.

> *You have to be very careful what you tolerate from others because you are teaching them how to treat you.*

When I was first starting to work with Tolerations, someone spoke to me in a way I found unacceptable. Before, I might have just let it go—maybe even have gotten into it with them in a similar temper.

This time, I told this individual that I no longer allowed people to talk to me in that fashion and ended the conversation.

In addition, I informed them that this type of exchange— if continued—would seriously damage our relationship.

It made a real difference. I think they respected me more for it. And I certainly felt better about myself.

You have to set the standard and stand up to people who exceed your boundaries of fairness and respectful treatment of yourself.

Action Steps

I recommend that you do some journaling—or at least make a list—of what Tolerations and lower-than-desired standards have cost you. How have they manifested? The more you can identify the pain, the easier it will be to raise the bar and eventually master Toleration Freedom.

Michael E. Angier

Chapter 5
Toleration Freedom

"Freedom lies in being bold."
—Robert Frost

Freedom Isn't Free

Once you realize the cost of putting up with Tolerations, you're going to be more easily motivated to eliminate them.

Conversely, when you realize how awesome your life will be when you refuse to allow Tolerations to weigh you down, you will find yourself hunting them down and killing them with the determination of a Viking warrior.

Envision, if you will, a stress-free life. Never getting upset. Having the calm demeanor and quiet focus of a Buddhist priest. An abundance of energy and vitality.

Is it possible?

Perhaps not *completely*. But I think you can come pretty close.

And it's guaranteed that you *won't* achieve it if you're burdened by Tolerations.

Michael E. Angier

Be Better Prepared

Certainly there are things outside of your control that happen to you and cause you to feel stressed. Some big—some small. But it's not what happens *to* you, it's how you *respond* to what happens to you that makes the difference. It's always what you think about what happens that determines your response.

And if you are Toleration free—or nearly so—you are much better prepared and far more capable of handling what comes down your path.

> *It's not what happens to us, it's how we respond to what happens to us.*

Would You Like More Confidence?

As you start knocking off your Tolerations, you are going to feel great. You're winning. And winning builds confidence and raises your belief level in your ability to accomplish even more. It's fun, too.

> *Winning builds confidence and raises your belief level in your ability to accomplish even more.*

As you knock off your small Tolerations, the bigger ones won't be so intimidating.

You know how it feels when you check off an item on your To Do list? Well that feeling is nothing compared to checking off an actual Toleration.

You feel more in charge and in control. You're ten feet tall and bullet-proof.

Say No to Overwhelm

OK, I can't promise that you'll *never* feel overwhelmed. Sometimes things can feel like they're too much to handle. But you will certainly experience *less* overwhelm. Simply because you're not dealing with as much as before.

You can take on challenges better, because you haven't been beaten up and beaten down as much as you were before by the accumulation of endless Tolerations.

Can You Be the Energizer Bunny?

There's only a certain amount of energy that you have in any given day. It can be enhanced by getting more or better sleep, proper diet and reduced alcohol consumption, to name a few.

And it can sometimes be artificially extended with caffeine and energy drinks. But at some point in any day, your energy is depleted—sometimes completely gone.

Toleration Freedom results in your energy not being drained unnecessarily. Simply being awake uses up physical and mental energy. And anything you can do that reduces the energy drain leaves you with more to enjoy and to be productive with.

Toleration extermination clearly allows you to have more energy.

And with more energy, you can learn more, do more, play more—and experience more of your Best Life.

---

*"The biggest adventure you can
take is to live the life of your
dreams."*

—Oprah Winfrey

How About More Creativity?

With more energy, better focus and less stress, you clear
the way to being more creative. There's more room for it
to flow.

By resolving and eliminating your aggravations, you invite
more creativity in. You open yourself to more of what life
has to offer.

Action Step

Spend some time visualizing your life with few, if any,
Tolerations. See yourself having an abundance of energy,
feeling powerful, confident—even blissful. Welcome to
Toleration Freedom.

Michael E. Angier

Chapter 6
Identifying Your Tolerations

"The first step toward change is awareness. The second step is acceptance."

—Nathaniel Brandon

Here's a list to help you look for areas of your life you may have Tolerations:

Personal Appearance

- hair
- weight
- fitness
- health
- teeth
- skin
- clothes
- grooming

Stressors

- business
- accounting
- money
- investments
- emotional issue

- taxes
- legal
- health

Home and Office

- size
- furniture
- safety/security
- location
- convenience
- newness
- comfort
- community
- noise level
- layout
- lighting
- beauty

Family & Relationships

- spouse
- relatives
- siblings
- parents
- children
- partners
- colleagues
- friends
- co-workers
- vendors
- neighbors

Car, Equipment

- appliances
- color
- age
- dependability
- cleanliness
- condition
- technology
- attractiveness/feel

Work

- compensation
- routine
- convenience
- challenge
- boss
- advancement
- role/responsibility

Feelings/Emotions

- anger
- hurt/sadness
- overall satisfaction
- loneliness
- overall happiness
- tiredness
- energy level

Lifestyle

- fun
- creativity

Michael E. Angier

- me-time
- eating habits
- sleeping habits
- regular check-ups
- energy levels
- stress level
- adventure

Finances

- debt
- insurance
- reserves
- retirement plan
- income
- taxes
- diversification

Integrity

- promises made/kept
- finances
- taxes
- confidences kept
- legal

Security

- wills
- living wills
- trusts
- self-defense

Community

- volunteering
- community service
- politics

This is by no means a complete list. Feel free to add to it. But it will certainly get you started in the right direction.

Action Steps

1. From the areas listed above, add at least 25 new Tolerations you thought of to your list.

2. Download this free Personal Achievement Assessment from SuccessNet at www.SuccessNet.org/psa

With it, you'll be able to evaluate yourself in many different areas of your life and find even more undiscovered Tolerations. Consider it your personal success inventory.

> *Give yourself a checkup from the neck up to see where you are in terms of your personal and professional development.*

Michael E. Angier

Chapter 7
Levels of Tolerations

"Action expresses priorities"
—Mahatma Gandhi

Big or Small, Destroy Them All

Obviously some Tolerations have more of an impact on your life than others. And you may be asking yourself how to prioritize them. Do you knock off the quick, easy ones and build up momentum and confidence to tackle the big hairy one?

Or do you go for the mean, nasty ones that, if fixed, could knock off some smaller ones like a bowling ball knocking down ten pins?

There's no right or wrong way to do it.

Sometimes They Breed

Oftentimes one Toleration is causing, creating or allowing some of the others to exist. So boldly knocking off one of those bad boys might very well be a priority.

But sometimes you don't know—until afterward—that a Toleration was a breeder. The game is to kill them all.

I find it helpful in prioritizing Tolerations if you can assign them to the following three levels.

Michael E. Angier

Level One

These are Tolerations that have serious ramifications in your life. If not handled, they will have dire consequences—sometimes deadly ones. Gross obesity, smoking, overdrinking, reckless behaviors and consistently living beyond your means are examples.

Level One's present real deterrents to you living your Best Life. They are things you must work to eliminate. Not doing so will cause severe consequences.

Level Two

Level Two's are important to eradicate. But they're not life threatening. They are things that have a negative impact on your productivity, your intended results, quality of life, finances, etc. The Tolerations in this category are things you are committed to exterminate, but might require some goal setting and project selection—maybe even some assistance—to get them handled.

Level Three

The Tolerations in this level are bothersome, but tolerable—at least for the moment. They are the items you have identified as irritating, annoying, unused, worn out, tarnished and obsolete—they are distracting, niggly, pesky Tolerations.

And individually, they might not seem like much at all. But as I've said, they add up. Add enough of them together and they are definitely dragging you down.

Often, these are quick and easy to eliminate. And they may be a good place to start to get your skill and confidence to the point where you can tackle the Level One's and Two's with more courage and belief in yourself.

Do not, however, underestimate the evil mayhem these Tolerations are capable of creating. Chances are, you have previously been aware of your Level One's—and hopefully already made progress on them. But the Level Three's are sneakier, less obvious—yet still dangerous. Like termites, they can do great damage to your "house" without being seen. And your first awareness of them can be a serious infestation—maybe even a collapse.

Action Step

Go through your list of Tolerations and mark them as Level 1, 2 and 3 as a way of categorizing and prioritizing them.

Michael E. Angier

Chapter 8
Four Ways of Dealing with Tolerations

---

*"Sometimes life knocks you on
your ass . . . get up, get up, get
up! Happiness is not the
absence of problems, it's the
ability to deal with them."*
—Steve Maraboli

Ready for Some Great News?

For many Tolerations, the mere act of identifying and
naming them as a Toleration is often all you have to do to
eliminate them. Others will require some planning and will
need to be dealt with over time. However, some of them
are super easy to knock off. You'll be surprised at how just
seeing something as a Toleration will make it almost
magically disappear.

Charles Kettering—yes, the same guy who invented the
electric starter—said, "A problem clearly stated is a
problem half-solved." I believe it. And with Tolerations,
recognizing and naming them, in many cases, means
they're more than half zapped.

*With Tolerations, recognizing
and naming them, in many
cases, means they're more than
half zapped.*

A number of times, my wife and I have reviewed our
Toleration List and noticed that some items have
effortlessly disappeared, and we can't think of anything we
consciously did to make them go away.

But for all the others, once you've identified them, you're
faced with basically only four ways to address them.

1. Dump It

You can forget about it. Just delete it because it's not
worth it. Consciously choosing to delete a minor
Toleration (at least for the time being) still leaves you in
charge.

Just be careful you are not Tolerating it. Make sure it's
something you're truly willing to accept. There's freedom
in deleting a potential Toleration. You can always come
back to it and reconsider—maybe after your standards
have risen from your mastery of Toleration Freedom.

2. Delegate It

Just because it's your Toleration, doesn't mean you have to
be the one to fix it. I contribute to the dirtiness and
disorder that happens in our house, but we pay someone
to clean it regularly. There's no shame in having someone
else take care of something you want dealt with.

You have to value your time. And usually, you can find someone who you can pay less than your hourly worth to take care of things that you don't want to do or don't have time for.

Take a look at www.Fiverr.com or www.UpWork.com for all the different kinds of things people can do for you remotely—and for very little cost. They may actually be able to eliminate some of your Tolerations. Or, perhaps they can do some of the things you're doing now that will free you up to slay these Toleration dragons on your own. Delegation is a powerful thing indeed.

3. Do It

If you can't delete it or delegate it—and don't be too quick to think you can't—you may just have to get 'er done on your own.

If you can't quite commit to handling it completely, commit to starting on it. Get the tools you need. Research it. Find out the best way to go about it. Tell yourself you will work on it for 20 minutes. When I've done this, I usually find myself working longer than the 20 minutes, or even 10 minutes I committed to working.

Do whatever it takes to make progress on zapping your Tolerations. It will get easier. You will get better at it. And you will like it. You really will.

4. Reframe It

Sometimes you can transform the way you see and experience a Toleration. How you view it can make a difference.

Michael E. Angier

I recently had what I thought might be a Toleration. A warning light appeared on the dashboard of my car telling me that the tire monitoring system was not fully operational. I was thinking of getting it fixed and found out it's about $100 per tire.

Well, the fact of the matter is, I keep a good eye on my tires. And the service tech at the dealership said that with the car being a few years old, I could expect to replace them more than once. Fix one, and soon another one will go.

So I decided to have the warning light remind me to check our tire pressure even more regularly than I had been doing. Instead of it being a Toleration, it's now a helpful reminder. I could have dealt with it with option one and deleted the Toleration from my list. Instead I chose number four and reframed it.

> *"To reframe something, step back from what is being said and done and consider the frame, or 'lens' through which this reality is being created."*
> —Changing Minds

Action Step

Go through your list again and see which ones you can dump, do, delegate or reframe.

Chapter 9
Fixing Your Tolerations

---

*"Worry a little bit every day
and in a lifetime you will lose a
couple of years. If something is
wrong, fix it if you can. But
train yourself not to worry:
Worry never fixes anything."*
—Ernest Hemingway

Without knowing what your particular Tolerations are, I cannot tell you exactly how to eliminate each one. They are too different. What I *can* do is give you some guidelines.

And as I said earlier, many of your Tolerations will be simple enough and small enough that you won't have to have a plan of action to get rid of them. The way to fix them will be obvious. Simply naming them, calling them for what they are, will make it easy to handle them.

By the way, I don't just delete them off my Toleration list when they are handled. I take them off the list and add them to my Toleration Win List. It's gratifying to see the Win List grow. And it's a nice visual to see our progress toward Toleration Freedom.

Michael E. Angier

Be Good to Yourself

A word of caution as you begin your campaign against your Tolerations: Don't make yourself wrong for having tolerated these things and not handled them sooner. It will do you no good. In fact, it could help to keep you stuck.

Instead, I encourage you to practice what I call *Correction Without Invalidation*.

Most of us waste a great deal of time and energy beating ourselves up over the mistakes we make. But you've reached real maturity when you can practice Correction Without Invalidation.

It's important that you acknowledge your errors and learn from them. But it does no good—in fact it's detrimental—to invalidate yourself. You need to refocus and not berate yourself—or others.

Correction Without Invalidation is a simple concept, and few would argue against its wisdom. But grasping a concept and living it in your life are two different things. I'm not saying it's easy. But I am saying it's worth mastering.

Winners spend little to no time being upset for not being further along or having made mistakes. They notice, they learn and they move on. They can dislike the sin (error) but continue to love and appreciate the sinner.

I don't believe in failure. You either win or you learn.

> *"If you haven't forgiven
> yourself for something, how can
> you forgive others?"*
> —Dolores Huerta

Tackle Them One at a Time

If you've been working at it—and you've been honest with yourself—your Tolerations List should be fairly lengthy by now.

Don't be intimidated by it. You don't need to go after them all at once. You didn't allow them into your life all at once, and you will not eradicate them all at once, either.

Yard by yard, life can be hard. But inch by inch, it's a cinch.

You may want to tackle the easy ones first to gain momentum and build confidence. And you may want to break the bigger ones down so they are more doable.

Action Step

Challenge yourself to handle three Tolerations within the next five to seven days. Make a game of it. Surely there are three you can knock off in the next week. And remember to celebrate eliminating them.

Michael E. Angier

Chapter 10
Roadblocks to Toleration Freedom

"You have to see every potential roadblock as an opportunity and a benefit."
—Suze Orman

The road to Toleration Freedom is never completed. It's always under construction. If you ever get through your whole Tolerations List (I never have), you'll find more to add to it as you travel through your life.

To be clear, I'm not advocating you spending all your life recognizing and eliminating Tolerations. What I'm saying is that you will have more of your life to live with more ease, comfort and joy by investing yourself in zapping these enemies of peace and tranquility.

As you get better and better at recognizing and eliminating Tolerations, you will be raising your standards. And things you didn't see as Tolerations before will become Tolerations because you are expecting and demanding more from life.

Here's what I've found to be the biggest challenges to continued success with this process. Being aware of them will help you live a life where things roll smoothly.

Having Standards That Are Too Low

Usually our standards are raised as we travel down the Toleration Freedom Road. But sometimes things happen in our life that cause us to slip back into old patterns. This certainly is something to be aware of, and if you start to slide, get back to standing up for what you deserve.

Not Believing It Matters That Much

We humans have a tendency to devalue ourselves too easily. We invalidate what we've done as "no big deal"— especially if it was easy. Please believe me when I tell you that this stuff really matters. And it will continue to matter if you remain diligent.

Not Taking It Seriously

I've done my best to show you how valuable Toleration Freedom can be and how much better your life can work by exterminating your Tolerations. And if you've gotten this far, you must think it has some merit.

You can have fun with it. You can laugh—and I think you should—at some of the silly Tolerations you have put up with. But do take it seriously.

Not Sticking With It

Remember that this is not something you do once and check it off as done. It's an ongoing endeavor. It's a way to continue to polish and up-level your life. It doesn't need to take a lot of time, but it is something you need to stick with.

> *"Patience, persistence and*
> *perspiration make an*
> *unbeatable combination for*
> *success."*
> —Napoleon Hill

Forgetting About It

I urge you to keep your Tolerations List **visible**—not tucked away in some out-of-the-way place. Out of sight is often out of mind. Incorporate your review of your Tolerations into your weekly, monthly and quarterly review process. You do have those kinds of meetings, right? Corporations do. And your life is certainly more important than a corporation.

Justifying Your Tolerations

Sometimes people are attached to their Tolerations—even claiming they are *not* Tolerations. Are you truly willing to accept it? Or are you making excuses for it. This process requires that you be completely honest with yourself.

I've done it. Turned a blind eye to something I wasn't willing to let go of. It's amazing how much in denial we will allow ourselves to be at times.

One thing that helps is to ask yourself how this particular "thing" is helping you. What's the pay-off of having it in your life?

It's all part of raising your standards.

Not Enlisting Support

This process is easier and more fun if you can do it with someone else. Consider enrolling your significant other in the game—unless they are one of your Tolerations. Work with a partner or a member of your master mind team.

Or find someone you know and trust and become accountabilibuddies for one another. I know that if I tell myself I'm going to accomplish something by Friday, there's a good chance it will get done. But if I tell my accountabilibuddy it will be done by Friday, it will for *sure* get done by Friday. Because he's going to ask me about it, and I don't ever want to say it didn't get done.

I've often said that if you can win the game by yourself, you probably aren't playing a big enough game. A big life, your *best* life, will be something that you cannot make happen on your own.

Action Step

Determine who you will work with on your Toleration Freedom. Find a friend, partner, spouse, co-worker and help each other sort through those Tolerations. Brainstorm ways to knock off the Level 3s and come up with goals and projects to take care of the Level 1s and 2s. Have fun with it. And celebrate your wins—big and small.

Chapter 11
Uncovering Even More Tolerations

"Whatever is now covered up
will be uncovered and every
secret will be made known."
—Melina Marchetta

Think You've Gotten Them All?

As you travel down the path of Toleration Freedom, you'll see that the more Tolerations you name, the more you will find. And you'll wonder why you didn't notice them before.

Even though you will discover them on your own, here are several proven-to-be-helpful processes that will help you uncover even more Tolerations and gain more clarity about lots of other things in your life.

SCOT Analysis

SCOT stands for Strengths, Challenges, Opportunities and Threats. You may have heard of it as SWOT, (with the W standing for weaknesses) but I didn't like weaknesses and replaced it with Challenges.

I maintain two ongoing SCOTs. One for my business and one for my life.

What are your **strengths**? What are you good at? What's working in your favor? Experience. Talents. Skills. Savings, etc. Put it all down and add to it over time.

What are your **challenges**? Big or small, list them all. What are the problems you face? Where do you not have an advantage? What causes you to hold back and not go for it? Of course, you will eventually figure out what you can do about these challenges.

What are your **opportunities**? What could you do that's available to you? Remember that you can do anything, you just can't do *everything*. So you'll need to choose carefully. This is the place to write them all down so you don't lose them.

What are the **threats**? What could become a problem for you? We certainly don't want to dwell on all the catastrophe that could come our way, but we don't want to bury our head in the sand either. Once we know what they are, we can insure, protect or prevent them from causing us harm.

WW/WD/WN

This acronym stands for What Worked? What Didn't? and What's Next?

I use it as a fallback agenda for almost any meeting. It's a great way to review a day, a week, a month, etc. It's very helpful in evaluating a project or goal. Or you can use the questions to see where your primary relationship stands: What's working? What isn't? Where do we want to go from here/

More/Less/Start/Stop

Going through this process will surely turn up a few items to place on your Tolerations List as well as help you to select goals, projects and tasks that support your Best Life Vision.

It's a simple process of listing what you want more of, or what you want to *do* more of. And then, what you want to have less of or do less of.

Then ask yourself what you would like to *start* doing that you're not doing currently.

And what you are doing that you would like to stop doing.

Action Step

I encourage you to try one or two of these processes and see how they work for you. They have certainly been helpful to me and many others for gaining greater clarity.

When you are clear, what you want in your life shows up. And the quality and quantity of what shows up is in direct proportion to your degree of clarity.

When you are clear, what you want in your life shows up. And the quality and quantity of what shows up is in direct proportion to your degree of clarity.

Michael E. Angier

Chapter 12
Commencement

---

*"Today, you have 100% of
your life left."*

—Tom Hopkins

Welcome To Your New Life

You've finished this book—almost. Congratulations!

It's been said that only ten percent of people who buy a non-fiction book read more than the first chapter. That sets you apart.

It may be the end of this book, but you're just beginning your life of Toleration Freedom—greater expectations, higher standards, smoother sailing, less stress and a more simplified existence. And, of course, more clarity.

This is not a one-and-done kind of deal. It's a constant and never-ending effort. And the longer you do it, the better you get. And the higher your standards become.

Sharpen The Saw

In Stephen Covey's great book, *The Seven Habits of Highly Effective People*, he talked about the importance of *Sharpening the Saw*. As Franklin Covey's website states, "Sharpen the Saw means preserving and enhancing the greatest asset you have—you. It means having a balanced program for self-renewal in the four areas of your life: physical, social/emotional, mental, and spiritual."

You now know how to Sharpen the Saw by recognizing Tolerations and eliminating them. It's a powerful tool for polishing and simplifying your life.

I wish you great success in mastering Toleration Freedom.

Action Step

Make a commitment to yourself that you won't quit. Take this on as a life-long challenge to making the rest of your life the best of your life.

A Thank You and a Request

Thank you for reading my book! I really appreciate all of your feedback, and I love hearing what you have to say.

I need your input to make the next version of this book—and my future books—better.

Please leave a brief and helpful review on Amazon to let me know what you thought of the book. Only about one in a thousand readers leave a review. I hope you will be a one-in-a-thousand reader.

You can use this link:
www.Amazon.com/dp/B07PPHVY7Z

Thank you very much.

Michael E. Angier

BeYourBest@SuccessNet.org
www.SuccessNet.org

About the Author

Michael E. Angier is the founder and CIO (Chief Inspiration Officer) of SuccessNet based in the Tampa Bay area of Florida. He's a father, grandfather, husband, writer, speaker, entrepreneur, coach and student.

He's the author of *101 Best Ways to Get Ahead, 101 Best Ways to Be Your Best, The Achievement Code, How to Create a Vivid Vision for Your Life* and others.

Michael's work has been featured in numerous publications such as *USA Today, Selling Power, Personal Excellence* and *Sales & Marketing Excellence* as well as dozens of electronic publications. He's been interviewed on both TV and radio many times.

His internationally popular articles have earned him a Paul Harris Fellowship with Rotary International.

Angier has experienced personal and professional success, but he's also suffered some bitter defeats. Although certainly preferring the former, he feels that he's learned the most from his struggles and disappointments. He feels that life's greatest lessons are learned by overcoming the obstacles in the path of a challenging and worthwhile objective.

Michael's passion is human potential. He believes fervently in the indomitable human spirit and revels in helping people and companies grow and prosper.

Over the past 40 years, Michael has devoted himself to studying what works and has been an ardent student of the principles of success. He's taught seminars and conducted workshops on goal setting, motivation and personal development in six countries.

Mr. Angier is a positive and optimistic man. He views the next few decades as a time of unparalleled change and incredible opportunity. He sees "high-tech" merging with "high-touch" in a way that could allow for personal and spiritual transformation to seem almost magical. He sees science and spirituality as complementary.

Michael feels that there are three things essential to living a fulfilling and successful life: a purpose to live for, a self to live with and a faith to live by.

Michael is married to Dawn Angier—his partner, best friend, mentor, teacher, student and confidante. They have six adult children and five grandchildren. Michael enjoys tennis, traveling, reading and helping people realize their dreams.

Michael E. Angier

Other Books by Michael Angier
www.Amazon.com/author/michaelangier

The Achievement Code
The 3C Formula for Getting What You Truly Want

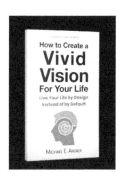

How to Create a Vivid Vision for Your Life
Live Your Life by Design Instead of by Default

Other Books by Michael Angier

www.Amazon.com/author/michaelangier

101 Best Ways to Be Your Best
Practical Wisdom to Maximize Your Unique Potential

101 Best Ways to Get Ahead
Solid Gold Advice from the World's Most Successful People

Mistakes Happen

We're committed to publishing inspiring, practical and professional books. However, mistakes do occur. If you should find a typographical or grammatical error, we would be most grateful to you for making us aware. And if you are the first to tell us about it, we'd be happy to send you a thank you gift.

Just eMail your find with the book name, location and type of error to BeYourBest@SuccessNet.org with "Found This!" in the subject. Thanks for your help.

Free Resources

Personal Achievement Assessment

Download this free tool from SuccessNet. With it, you'll be able to evaluate yourself in many different areas of your life and find even more undiscovered Tolerations. Consider it your personal success inventory (PDF).

www.SuccessNet.org/psa

How to Write a Motivating Mission Statement

A clear purpose is the foundation for your success. This Smart Guide includes examples of both personal and organization mission statements (PDF).

www.SuccessNet.org/mission

Report: Raising the Bar

Increase your standards of excellence. Your special report may be downloaded at

www.SuccessNet.org/files/raisethebar.pdf

Michael E. Angier

Acknowledgements

I thank my wife, Dawn, who is my business and life partner as well as my best friend. She provided not only encouragement and feedback, but also her highly professional copy editing and technical expertise. She always makes me—and my work—look better.

I'd also like to thank some folks who participated in a beta class on this topic. This book is better organized as a result of their faith in me and their interest in identifying and getting rid of their Tolerations. They are Sandi Neilson, Mike Ward, Andrew Freundlich, Christine Cox, Ed Jamison, Jerry Pinney, Patrick O'Loghlen, Andreea Cruceru and Scott McAfoos.

Lastly, I wish to thank the tens of thousands of subscribers and members of SuccessNet, who over the past 24 years, have followed me and supported our efforts in helping us all create and live our Best Lives. They are a great source of inspiration to me. And their patronage has allowed me to do work that I love for over two decades.

Made in the USA
Las Vegas, NV
29 July 2021